"Rachel" —

"May your joys

be truly "Gingham Joys"

Love,

Pearl

Gingham Joys

MARION
FLOOD
FRENCH

ingham Joys

ABINGDON PRESS

NEW YORK
NASHVILLE

GINGHAM JOYS

Copyright © 1962 by Abingdon Press

Library of Congress Catalog Card Number: 62-7226

B

SET UP, PRINTED, AND BOUND BY THE
PARTHENON PRESS, AT NASHVILLE,
TENNESSEE, UNITED STATES OF AMERICA

THIS BOOK IS DEDICATED TO MY DEAREST
and to those people, places,
and ideas which have given
me my *gingham joys*

The first lesson a newspaper writer learns is brevity. But how does one say "Thank you" in two paragraphs? There is Jack Moran, managing editor, *Bangor Daily News,* whose imaginative foresight saw the possibilities of service through daily "Lenten Windows" from which this book was adapted. There is Richard K. Warren, publisher, *Bangor Daily News,* whose warm encouragement and friendliness make possible this kind of effort. There are all the people near and far who have called, commented, and

Preface written about the column, which still appears each Lenten season in this newspaper. . . . . .

Perhaps the best way is to say that the spirit and intention embodied in *Gingham Joys* has been given to me a

thousandfold through my six-
teen years as a member of the
Bangor Daily News family.
Were it not for this organization's vision and ideals this
book would not be. . . . . .

MARION FLOOD FRENCH

Contents

Gingham Joys

  * Sometimes when we are house- or office-bound for a very long period of time we begin to think of joy as something dissociated from our everyday manner of living. It has to be different before we see it.

But there are joys all around us, quiet ones. Call them gingham joys because they are so familiar. What might they be?

A valentine morning, lacy, white, and cold; sunlight in a scrubbed and quiet house; the security and shelter of a home on a stormy night; lamplight on your loved one's face; the merry, perceptive remarks of a child unbound by social strictures; the friendly smiles on the faces of those you know only by the common bond of daily passing by. . . . . .

The river on an autumn afternoon, the changing seasons on a landmark grown so near you seldom see it, copper on a wall, rainbows from the neon lights on a rainy night. . . . . .

Gingham joys—quiet ones, common ones. Collect them wherever you can. Wear them in a smile that begins in your eyes. Wear them with pride for they are the fiber of life, deep and warm and dear. And they are yours.

GINGHAM JOYS BELONG TO ALL WHO SEE WITH THE HEART

The Fires of Happiness

* We have all dreamily watched a fire burning in a grate and have seen there pictures of our dreams. A hearthfire presents another picture too. Did you ever think how much like happiness it is?

The leaping flame...... there is a happiness like that. It's a spring thing...... a prerogative of youth. This temper of spirit, this leaping abandon becomes the young......

Then there is the steady glow. It comes when the fiber of the fire is right, seasoned, planned, placed just so, chosen for the sure and steady heat it provides. This radiance and security reach out to envelop all our loved ones, to give strength and comfort. That's happiness, too......

Easiest to watch, strongest in radiance, the foundation of the fire, are the coals. These are contentment, companionship, trust. As long as these exist there is, as with the coals of the fire, a promise of leaping flame, for coals have the power to kindle anew.

And what of the sparks which fly upward? The bits of flame that build a blaze wherever they light? This is the love you share with others. It is to say that you have more than enough and to share.

The fires of happiness. . . . . . flames, steadfastness, contentment, sparks. Have you built your fire this way?

SOMEONE HAS SAID, "THE HEARTHSTONE WAS THE WORLD'S FIRST ALTAR."

Querencia

* Out of a Spain of sun and sand, out of a sport both brutal and bloody, comes a word which can bring peace to a heart. . . . . . *querencia.*

Querencia. . . . . . the spot to which the bull retreats again and again when he senses this is the struggle to death.

Everyone of us has a *querencia.* . . . . . or wants to. To each heart there comes a time of retreat. . . . . . for renewal. It may be to a place, to a memory, to a moment. It may be in listening to the long silver note of a shining trumpet or to the sweet wet tapping of the rain. . . . . .

It may be our *querencia* is a person. Then we must beware lest our pause is unprotected ground, as it is for the uncomprehending bull, for rare is the soul who does not have his own need for refuge and in that need break beneath our leaning.

But if your *querencia* is a moment of faith then it becomes truly a hiding place. . . . . . a source of renewal fresh as the morning, soft as the sunset, eternal as the cycle of our planet.

Querencia. . . . . . we all need it. Love does provide it sometimes. . . . . . but the kind of love which assures it must be divine.

MAKE YOUR QUERENCIA A
MOMENT WITH GOD.

Hyacinths

          * If ever there were advice which appeared to slash across the American reputation for practicality it is that of the ancient one who said, "Buy hyacinths to feed the soul."

Yet I wonder if things are as they seem. Everyone needs hyacinths to feed the soul. And everyone has them. It may be books, tier upon tier. It may be a painting, strong in line, in color, which speaks only to you. It may be the memory of a raw October night which holds the smoke of bonfires or of a rose-lit summer morning with houses still frosted by the night's chill. It may be a busy city bridge seen in the dawn of a new workday, a street you visit once a year and remember that it has heard echoing footsteps through the centuries.

In every region where nature seems to go to extremes hyacinths may be hidden but they are there. Nor should we become apologetic for seeking flowers for our spirits. Be happy for those moments of grace—the forsythia tree whose progress you watch in the warm, sweet days of spring; the valentine noses of small white kittens; the outflung hand of a sleeping child; small birds' wings fluttering.

What comes to us if we dare to search for hyacinths to feed our souls? Vision and strength to face the gray day.

> NONE OF US IS SO POOR HE CANNOT AFFORD A SPIRITUAL BOUQUET.

We All Like to Go Back

        * We all like to go back to memories of other days. Maybe to a small white church overlooking a blue bay, maybe to a family sing, or maybe to some small bit of preciousness that we have carried in our hearts for many years. As our days add up we are inclined to gloss over the actuality and remember only the happiness involved. But the actuality does remain deep within us, sleeping, and it accounts for many of the inexplicable things we do. That is why the making of a memory is so important.

What kind of memories are you making? For yourself? For your children? What do you want them to remember? A pleased look that parents exchange silently, unaware that children sense the pleasure? A sure knowledge that a family is united and can withstand the storms of living? A faith that is exemplified in the only way a child can understand. . . . . . in his parents?

Memories are made by awareness of life in its beauty and in its pain, by steady thought one for the other in all our associations. You can paint a gray picture of bickering, nagging, and complaint, or you can paint a gay picture of gallantry beyond the call of duty. We all have that choice.

Whether we are poor or rich, comfortable or ill at ease, we have the privilege of choosing the pattern which will grace our future days, which will clothe our hearts and minds with ease or dis-ease. We all like to go back. . . . . .

WHAT KIND OF MEMORIES
ARE YOU MAKING TODAY?

What's the Matter with Corn?

> * One of the most devastating, supposedly, of criticisms by the sophisticate is, "It's corn!"

So—what's the matter with corn? Really now, did you ever stop to think, America was built on it? Through all our history both practically and sentimentally we have taken the unabashed emotional way when the going got rough. Through depression, war, and peace the things that spoke clearest to us spoke in words that would be termed "corny" by the sophisticated. But we heard those words and took them to heart.

Take Christmas. Christmas is a time of unabashed sentiment—the carols, the trees, the gifts, the traditions. The story as we know it could not possibly have come from a more humble origin. A story that common people heard gladly, a story with musical accompaniment, a story with that most emotional of centers—a tiny babe. But it held the heart of the world.

So the next time you freeze before sentiment, the next time you hesitate before something which seems "corny," stop and think before you condemn. Ask yourself, "What's the matter with corn?"

SIMPLICITY IS NOT SENTIMEN-
TALITY; SIMPLICITY IS TRUTH.

Reading the Label

* I know a gal who cooks from the labels on boxes quite frequently, and the result is delicious. That is worthy of comment here only because it is rarer than you might think. Most of us feel that the traditional approach is best. It might be. But it is not the only approach. Any good cook knows that one is adventuring when one goes beyond the rule book. Yet adventuring is good for the spirit.

Without a willingness to adventure we soon fall into a rut and into blindness. You do not think so? How long since you have seen a new recipe on a label and have dared to try it?

Did you ever watch a child who is just learning to read? What escapes those eager eyes? Box tops and sides, signs, letters, the least small evidence of a chance to test this new skill is not missed. He is aware. He is eager.

He is anxious. He is full of the thrill of accomplishment.

We say we are beyond the thrill of new discovery. But are we? Must new discovery be only those blazing accomplishments which make first of all a monetary demand? Isn't cooking from box tops, hanging the curtains a new way, designing a pattern, just as much of an adventure?

The only demand this makes upon you is a willingness to experiment. Its success is not so important as the fact that suddenly you are reading labels again.

YOU DO NOT HAVE TO GO FAR AFIELD TO FIND ADVENTURE. IT IS AS NEAR AS YOUR KITCHEN CUPBOARD.

Two Kinds of Success

* Two people from the same background, bound with the same ties, finding the same joys, starting with the same opportunities. . . . . . One grows and acclaim comes to him, not just from his own community, but from the entire nation—money, fame, popularity. The other builds no bonfires. He is known, respected, and liked among his own. He has enough sustenance for peace of mind. He finds satisfaction in his daily task.

Did you ever think that you cannot say that one is more successful than the other? You cannot, for the finest kind of happiness is that which we find within our own spirits.

The man of fame may, indeed, be worthy of acclaim. But the man of home is equal in his success. It is no easy task to achieve small success. The magnitude of each endeavor is balanced.

To walk down Main Street knowing that you find happiness and contentment in gaining your daily bread, in greeting your neighbors, in being known but to a few, but being truly known, should make a man walk tall.

And the other, known to many? He can be proud too. But his pride should be for the same reasons. Happiness, contentment. . . . . .

There are two kinds of success, perhaps, as the world judges. But there is, in the truest analysis, only this one reward.

> SUCCESS WALKS DOWN ANY
> STREET IF YOU RECOGNIZE
> ITS REWARDS.

Choose Your Partners

            * It is fun to choose part-
ners at a square dance.
Usually we do this upon the basis of the bal-
ance, skill, and pleasure they will provide.
Sometimes we are not so wise when we choose
partners of the heart and spirit. . . . . .

A poor choice of a partner in a dance is not
a matter of too great moment. A dance doesn't
last that long. Yet a succession of poor partners can spoil your party. And partners who
occupy your heart and mind make for a very
long party, indeed.

Do you choose gaiety and good will? Or
irritation and gloom? Distrust or faith? It
would not be true to say that your choice does
not affect those around you. Of course it does.
But whether you choose to chip away at those
around you, at their warmth, their love, their
poise, is still not the greatest damage.

The greatest damage occurs within yourself. You are willfully spoiling your own party. Do you choose bickering or peace, in the name of happiness? Do you choose imposition or compromise, in the name of love?

Make no mistake. You do choose one way or another. The kind of party you have is entirely up to you.

YOU HAVE THE RIGHT TO
CHOOSE YOUR PARTNERS
EACH NEW DAY.

Whose Happiness?

            * We are inclined to pat ourselves on the back over the ways in which we handle happiness. We seldom admit that the happiness we are most concerned about is our own. We are more inclined to say, "I did it for her sake or for his sake, for my children, for a relative." We may be quite sincere in that evaluation.

Yet happiness is a tricky matter. It's a matter of thought that might well give us pause. That shining house you insist upon—is it for your family's comfort or your own preference? That story your friend has so much fun telling—are you really concerned about his exaggeration, or are you delighting in your own preciseness?

How many times have you used the excuse of love to demand? To impose? Whose happiness are you satisfying?

Happiness that comes from satisfactions of

physical comfort is a happiness which is short and shallow. Happiness which you give freely to others is deep and enduring.

The next time you find yourself claiming an action in the name of happiness ask yourself, "Whose happiness?"

THE EASIEST PERSON TO DE-CEIVE IS ONESELF—AND THE HARDEST TOO.

Heroes Do Not Make History

* The star complex is not new to contemporary life. Throughout time, in this country and others we have reserved a special place of honor for those who have performed heroic deeds and so we say "made history."

But heroes, alone, do not make history. People do that. Without the people to follow, to assess, to place their blessing upon the leadership of others, there would be no history as we know it. No Moses, no David, and forget it not . . . . . . no Hitler.

It is we common folk—you and me—and our children and theirs—who shape civilization. That puts a rather heavy burden, or if you prefer to think of it that way, blessing, upon our daily tasks.

That is why our attention to newsworthy events, to daily occurrences within our community, is so important. That is why we consider the teaching of citizenship to be more than a course in curricula.

You are shaping civilization—in the way in which you celebrate national and spiritual events, in the manner in which you serve, in the way in which you earn your daily bread, and in the way you love, or leave, your fellow man.

Heroes do not make history. They only sum it up. How do those ancient words go?

> The hopes and fears of all the years
> Are met in thee tonight.

IT IS YOU AND I WHO MAKE HEROES POSSIBLE. ARE YOU MAKING THE RIGHT CHOICE?

Country Style

        * Pages upon pages, pro and con, have been written about "the good old days." Yet as values and standards change, we must change, or we remain forever children caught in a world that never was.

One of the sturdy values of "country-style" living was an awareness of the needs of others. That such an awareness still exists, we sense, whenever we read of small community projects undertaken to meet the emergency needs of others. Usually whether city-size or small-town size these emergencies concern our neighbors.

Today our neighbors are the world, because the world is steadily shrinking within our concept. Yet the world sometimes fails to mean "people" to you and me.

The excuse of not having the time is a poor one for forgetting to help others, for it is not the big, demanding help that "country style" expects. How much time does it take to smile? That helps, you know. How much time does it take to ask after others? That is balm, you know. How much time, to say thank you?

It is sure as can be that there are things in country-style living that are better left in the past. Yet when we toss some things away we should do a careful job of sorting. It would be tragic to unknowingly throw out a treasure. And some essentials of country-style thinking are just that—treasures.

Most of us are fortunate enough to live "betwixt and between"—away from the cold concern of the city, within the warm convenience of the small town. We can make that warmth still warmer by extending a friendly hand, country style.

COUNTRY STYLE MEANS YOU CARE.

The Winner Stands Alone

* Colorful commercial wrestling to the contrary, the great wrestling matches of life are not always waged with explosive fury and trick holds. They are more often a matter of silent wrestling in a dark night of loneliness. And your stubborn opponent is fear—fear of failure, fear of inability to cope, fear of being alone. This last foe demands all your intelligence and skill because it is a human foe.

There is something basic and divine in standing alone. There is something proportionately magnificent in conquering your fear of it. Think how many times you do what you must, alone.

You must make decisions alone. No one else can face your pain, your troubles. No one else can take over your responsibilities in just your way. But, too, no one else can savor your joy, your peace of mind.

It is natural enough to want to escape at times. It is healthy to do just that . . . . . so long as it is a casual thing. It is when we depend upon escape that it becomes an instrument of the dark. Because then you lose its healing. The battle has to begin all over again.

If you have ever seen a bona fide, non-commercial, wrestling match fought in silent and matched skill, you will not soon forget its thrilling beauty. Nor will you ever again fear standing alone, for God intended that you should conquer that fear and that you should discover a paradox of life: There is always a cheering crowd and someone near to hold up your winning hand.

IF YOU WANT SOMEONE TO HOLD UP YOUR HAND YOU MUST WIN THE BATTLE ALONE.

The Three R's

       * Every time there is an upheaval over the state of education people stress going back to the three R's that symbolize the fundamentals of learning.

Coach Red Auerbach once listed the three R's of basketball, and in so doing, handed out a formula for success in daily living. The three R's he listed for top-notch performance on the basketball court were run, reach, and rebound.

Think about that. Is it not important that we pick up any task life hands us and in a sense "run" with it? The first enthusiasm which we bear for any challenge can carry us a long way forward, whether in the kitchen, in the office, or at school. Our initial momentum determines to great extent how smoothly our work will go.

Our reach is also important. All of us have

secret dreams of where our work will take us. We should not let those dreams fade, for dreams are dynamite.

Most vital of all is rebound. The mark of a whole personality is not success but striving —not that you fell but that you scrambled up again. If you can take things that *are* and reshape them into what should be you will be far more competent and secure. To be able to rebound is to hold the elasticity of spirit that laughs at time. It is the spirit that makes a champion.

> THE THREE R'S FOR THE GAME OF LIVING: RUN, REACH, AND REBOUND.

Condensed or Complete

   * The vogue today is for time saving. Did you ever ask yourself, why? What do you do with the time saved? An entire new field of books has grown up around this modern idea. Cut it, condense it, save time. Then we circle around to a field of writing designed to tell us what to do with our spare time.

Condensations, of course, serve a very worthy purpose, but they can become insidious to our mentality. A habit quickly entrenches itself. Ask any primary teacher who must constantly talk simply to her tiny charges how quickly it becomes a struggle not to express herself that way when she is talking with adults. With the condensation of speech comes, too soon, the condensation of thought.

This habit reaches, if we are not on guard, down into our spirits, our attitudes, our reactions. Then when we are confronted with a problem we find we are out of touch with the dimensional picture that shows the problem whole.

Certainly, read condensed books. But once in a while read a work in its entirety. You may not agree with what an editor considers is the meat of the matter. Of course, learn to outline a specific problem. But do not forget how to base it upon the broader background. Indeed, make a capsule prayer. But once in a while, kneel, and say our Lord's prayer— complete, not a condensation.

> THE SPIRIT IS NOT GIVEN TO CONDENSATION.

All the Colors

       * When the world puts aside her summer, which is frenetic for so many of her people, even the land seems to join in riotous release. In many places even her darkest roads and densest trails become avenues of light and lanes of fire.

There is so much in the way of harvest. There is so much in terms of color. No scraggly bush is ignored. No tall maple is spared. No one says, "This year we'll do every other tree. . . . . . This year we'll thin down our love." The color, be it light, as it sometimes is, or dark and glowing, is never less. The color—the spirit.

Sometimes when we view the blinding beauty of the harvest we shadow the moment by thinking ahead to the bareness, the cold, the snow, so soon to come. We make it a symbol of despair.

I wonder. . . . . . The snow is a comforter of white. White. . . . . . For rest, renewal, refreshment; white for purity, the kind of purity you knew in your childhood, in your faith.

White is the symbol of hope, not despair. The color is not gone. Remember? Remember your definitions?

White is not the absence of color. Ask any artist. White is where all colors are. . . . . .

SYMBOLS STAND FOR TRUTH.
BE SURE YOU SEEK OUT THAT
TRUE MEANING.

Taking Is Giving

* All of us have had the experience of feeling humble over receiving a gift. Sometimes it is not a pleasant experience. Most especially is this true when we are not in a position to return such an offering. Did you ever stop to think that taking is giving too?

If you ever reach a point in life where pride becomes a barrier to graceful receiving, think on that. People give to express a need just as much as people take because they need.

A child needs to give a gift at Christmas time that is "all his own" just as much as an older person does. An older person, financially limited, needs to give out of his limitation just as much as the one in a position to afford it.

There are seasons of the year when we become weary with giving. There are times of life when we are weary with receiving because it is hardest of all to take what we cannot return. But when, and all of us at times come up against this, we are faced with a favor which we cannot repay, remember that receiving graciously is giving too. It is the giving of self-respect which no person can afford to lose. . . . . .

ACCEPT THAT WELL-MEANT GIFT HAPPILY, FOR TAKING IS GIVING TOO.

There's Got to Be an Audience

* Sometimes we grow discouraged before the seeming successes of others—the stars of our small world. But did you ever stop to think there has to be an audience before there can be stars?

People do their best work, performers give that extra sparkle, before an enthusiastic group of people who acclaim. Without followers there would be no point in being a leader.

It may be that your forte lies in being a follower—the finest type of follower that you can be. We are not all temperamentally suited for the bright light of publicity and leadership.

The world and its fortunes often swing upon the combined force of public opinion. Opinion which is made up of the daily thoughts and actions of many, many people like you and me.

You hold a very vital force in your hands if you are a follower. You shape and form and mold the truth of this generation as you lead your child, as you teach your pupils, as you nudge shoulders with your neighbor and co-worker.

To be a part of an audience is one of the strength-giving blessings of this life. You have a chance for happiness that the lonely, glittering, few never have. If you are a follower count yourself blessed. And once in a while ask yourself this big question:

> WHAT KIND OF AUDIENCE AM I?

Candle in the Market Place

           * Most of us at one time or another have had a dream of burning a candle brightly in a select and noticeable place. Then as the years fly by we realize that such a spectacular accomplishment is not to be ours.

Instead of being the sergeant we become the privates. Maybe foot soldiers at that. But this does not mean we should allow our candles to burn out. It means, rather, that we should shield their small flames against the winds of adversity.

These winds of adversity are cynicism, defeat, and despair. They are indifference, carelessness, and wrong direction. It takes quick and clever juggling to keep these strong winds from blowing our candle flames out.

. . . . .

They are so strong and so many. The greatest struggle you can know, and the most magnificent, lies in the truth that so many do carry their candles to the market place. If you are engaged in that struggle you should feel the companionship of the past and the partnership of the present.

In your hello, your smile, your warm hand of help, show that you are proud of this partnership. It is the partnership of common men everywhere. Strong men, hopeful men, believing men. . . . . . Those bring their candles to the everyday market place.

MANY CANDLES MAKE A GREAT LIGHT.

Look Out Another Window

        * It is human nature to want to be where we are not. The harassed housewife envies her working sister. She sees only the freedom to leave the dishes or to buy a new dress. Her working friend envies the housewife's apparent security, forgetting that security demands responsibility and sacrifice. . . . . .

The outdoor worker envies the man at the desk, forgetting there are no time clocks on desks; and the other forgets the discontent which was his when he was told what to do and when. . . . . .

Look out another window when you hastily conclude the other view is best. Happy indeed is the man or woman who is aware of the values of his choice, for we all must choose, and if you have chosen time clocks then count the blessings they may bring, and if you have chosen creativity then bless the demands it makes upon you. . . . . .

We have done a disservice by phrasing the question, "Do you intend to have a career or to be a housewife?" We should say, "Which career do you choose?" We should not say, "How much money do you want to make?" We should say, "What do you demand of your job?" And when we have decided the question, the best cure for those human, envious hours is to look out another window.

> REFRESH YOUR HEART WHEN YOU ARE SATIATED WITH YOUR WORK BY LOOKING THROUGH ANOTHER WINDOW.

If You Only Have a Minute

    * If you only have a min-
    ute to drop in upon a be-
loved friend would you think of spending that
minute in complaining or making a request?
Think of those brief visits which all of us find
time to make. Do we not seek, in them, to
bring joy or liveliness to those upon whom we
call. And do we not, then, find our own lives
more joyful?

Then why not with God? Why not in the
brief visits which all of us find time to make
with him, make these too an occasion for re-
joicing, for saying thank you, for just linger-
ing in his presence with gratitude?

Too often we turn to him, informally, only
when in peril, despair, and grief. Is he a lesser
friend to you?

Did you ever think of turning to him when
you only have a minute? When you are dish-
washing, filing, typing? When you are taking

a coffee break or tucking a small elbow in it is very easy to say simply, "Thank you, God."

These are prayer beads—brief visits which will leave you with as much joy as a visit with another friend. And don't forget, you don't complain when you only have a minute.

> WE SURROUND OURSELVES
> WITH TOO MUCH FORMALISM.
> WHEN WE ONLY HAVE A MIN-
> UTE, WE CAN STILL THINK OF
> HIM.

Grace Notes

     * Grace notes are those small and unessential trills which embellish a piece of music but are not fundamentally necessary to the basic melody. Yet how nice they are to hear. They say that the composer took time to bring charm and beauty to the work he created. They speak of intent and an intrinsic love of finesse.

Do you put grace notes in your life? Do you say to all with whom you come in contact that you intend, whatever your estate, to live with a certain amount of grace?

Or do you say,"I'm still in the cave-man era."

We first think of grace notes as a matter of manners—the candle on the table, the escort to the door, the please and thank you of casual contact. But true grace notes go deeper than that.

They lie in the twinkle of the eye, the

warmth of your greeting, the intensity of your listening, the depth of your response.

They lie in the humor you find in living, the care you bring to your conversation. They lie in the personal touch. They are extras. They say this person is serene. They say this person takes time to bring beauty and charm to this life. What are your grace notes?

> EVERY COMPOSER USES GRACE NOTES. YOU ARE THE COMPOSER OF YOUR OWN LIFE.

Country Color

       * We are inclined to think of winter as a time of bleakness. The picture seems to be stark black and white. But it is not so. Have you ever truly looked at the countryside on a sunny winter day? A windswept field lies beige and blue and gold upon the landscape. The dead hay was never more brilliantly yellow against the white. The sun and sky were never more sharp and bright.

There are green and red roofs, pink and yellow houses, blue cottages just over the rise. They are sprinkled over the landscape like confetti in their gaiety of color. All the birches which we call silver in summer are white as driftwood in their slender simplicity. Each woods road wears a graceful mantilla of black lace as the humble bushes etch themselves against the barren background.

This kind of palette we never see in the

warm, full season. Then all blends together to make a tapestry rich and intricate—so intricate that the beauty of the individual may not be apparent.

So it may be with the barren times of life. Just as a jeweler displays a single gem to show more truly its fire and depth, so perhaps you are singled out that the true design may be evident.

THE COLOR LIES ALL AROUND US. IT TAKES WINTER TO SHOW IT TO THE WORLD.

What Do They Have?

       * Someone has said that Americans make a royalty of show-business people. Did you ever stop to think why? There are reasons. We speak of the ones who endure, not the shooting stars. These, almost always, have common denominators. . . . . .

First they achieve. They are a symbol to us of the possibility of making youthful dreams come true. . . . . .

Second they give. Their entire reason for being, for their dream, involves the giving of their gifts. In a fine fervor of abandon the great ones lose themselves for those they do not know. . . . . . And in the losing they find.

They intend to go on giving. They cannot conceive of the time when they will not be asking themselves, "What's next?" They do not recognize man-made barriers called years. . . . . .

Neither do they recognize man-made barriers of society. This does not mean they are undisciplined—not the ones who endure. They shape their lives to the deepest kind of discipline—to service. But they do not say service to this one, that type, this class, that color. They give to all who can laugh or cry, or hope, or despair.

We make a kind of royalty, they say, of the great ones. Try making a royalty out of the reasons for their success. Try giving, try devotion, try looking ahead, try discipline. The crown would fit your head, too, with this kind of shaping.

PUT A LITTLE STARDUST IN YOUR OWN LIFE.

Winter Windows

* It was so lovely we turned the car and went back to look at it again. The stream flowing softly in gentle curves was completely sheltered under smooth unbroken white. Not a track marred its sheen, and only the winter sun had penciled charcoal shadows from the trees along its banks. It lay in a small valley between two house-topped ridges. Still, serene, exquisite. It was a winter window.

And we wondered if the people in those two busy houses saw it so. So often one does not. The windows which lie close at hand we ignore. And then we fret, for we all do need a changing view. But often our idea is that the view must be different when actually all we need to do is view it differently.

Experiment with a small adventure. Pick some scene which has grown so familiar you hardly see it any more and study it. Watch what the changing days and seasons do to it. It does not have to be a grandiose view in the formal sense. It can be the back yard, the way the sun or rain or clouds bring moving colors to your street. Somewhere there is a poem about an invalid in the city whose only view from his tenement window was a patch of sky. The pleasure he found in this view would make you humble—and aware.

We need windows—particularly in a snowbound time of the soul. Of course we do. But sometimes we have them, and we don't take the time to look.

IS IT WINTER IN YOUR SPIRIT? SEARCH OUT A WINDOW AND WATCH SPRING ARRIVE.

Without a Score

* It is given to some of us to find our way through life without a score—without that written guidepost which musicians use to learn a particular masterpiece. This is frightening for any age, but for the very young who have to meet the problems of growing up it is a doubly difficult challenge to meet.

Yet it has been done, time after time. And you emerge from the experience the stronger for it—more sensitive too. For you learn early to think, to interpret, and to add to the pattern you see around yourself. You find new beauty because you can lift your eyes from an established pattern. You observe the small, the detailed, the intricate wonders of living.

And you learn, too, wherein your strength and the strength of all men lies. In the Source of all life.

There are times of loneliness, but you learn

to share the loneliness of others. There are times of triumph, but you learn to share that triumph. Just as you cannot lean, so you are not bound by tradition—by rigidity. You may become, because of this very tempering, one of the few who can interpret faith and strength to others.

It is no fun to play it without a score. But if for you, that must be, then never forget:

> THE GREATEST CONDUCTORS
> PLAY WITHOUT A SCORE.

Fences

* Did you ever notice as you ride down forgotten country lanes what is left of the love and laughter they once knew? Not houses—not many at least. Not pasture land, cleared and clean as it once was. Not flowers even. Not anything of love and care. These things have returned to God who gave them. And the land lies serene and lovely under his sky. Or would—but for fences. Fences—man-made to mark man's dominion. Shutting in his work, his love, his possessions. Shouting his pride of ownership. Shutting out the encroaching world, the strange ideas, that which he cannot touch or change, the extra, the difficult, the alien.

Saying, "This much I can do and no more."

Saying, "Within this enclosure lies all that I am or hope to be. Do not intrude. Do not ask me for more."

Fences. These remain to mar the land. They do not return, for they are not God-given. Nor is the spirit that built them—the spirit of pride, possession, fear. Enclosure. Exclusion. Fences. Man-made.

TODAY IS A GOOD TIME TO KNOCK DOWN FENCES.

The Forgotten Phrase

* There is a sturdy, old-fashioned New England phrase which has been pushed aside in late years. For some time now the furor and excitement in all areas of life have been for better human relations. The employer tippy-toes around the feelings of his employees; teachers cajole pupils; parents worry about damaging a child's personality with positive discipline. Such concern is good to a degree but fallacious if we think for a whit that it stems from love.

Genuine love, to promote growth, must be reciprocal. Successful human relationships are built upon that fact.

Why not, for a change, focus upon that sturdy old phrase we've nearly forgotten: Built upon honor? Instead of concentrating upon the outstretched hand, why not become the hand which turns to the job before us and does it well, as our forebears did? As an employee pour honor into the work you do. As a teacher stand upon your teaching. As a parent teach your child to build upon honor.

If we recall this forgotten phrase, which was in the fiber of our forebears' being, then perhaps unwieldy human relationships will fall into place. For although our Lord admonished us to love our neighbors he also said, "Well done, thou good and faithful servant: thou hast been faithful over a few things, I will make thee ruler over many things: enter thou into the joy of thy lord."

TODAY SAY PROUDLY OF WHATEVER JOB YOU UNDERTAKE: BUILT UPON HONOR.

The Most Important Part

* A Sunday-school teacher asked her small pupils what they considered to be the most important part of the Lord's Prayer. Bright-eyed Pete piped up, "The amen."

He wasn't old enough to realize it, but he was right. Because the word "amen" roughly translated means "as you will." "So be it." We make our prayer but we end it by saying "as you will." We commit our wishes and our dreams to his care and judgment. This is not an easy thing to do even in our closest human relationships.

How many times have you been unwilling to let an argument or a misunderstanding rest? How many times have you allowed a neighborhood quarrel to burgeon into a community scandal simply because you could not say amen? How much serenity and peace of mind have you lost because, after doing the best that you could, you have not learned to say amen? So be it.

This quality is even more difficult for young people to attain, for youth is enthusiastic over the swift pace of life. But before the next big exam, after you have studied your heaviest, try saying with devotion, "Amen." See if in the crucial moment your thoughts do not come clearer, stronger, and more correctly.

T. S. Eliot put it this way: "For us, there is only the trying. The rest is not our business." [1] As Christians we have this reminder every day. Try as you move about your business to send that Christian blessing after each task.

> DON'T JUST SAY "AMEN."
> PRAY IT. IT IS THE MOST IM-
> PORTANT PART OF YOUR
> PRAYER.

[1] From "East Coker" in *Four Quartets,* copyright, 1943, by T. S. Eliot. Reprinted by permission of Harcourt, Brace & World, Inc. and Faber and Faber, Ltd.

Mink or Mouton

      * To most of us, men as well as women, mink has come to symbolize the epitome of quality. We would all like mink. Most of us settle for mouton. We don't have to make that settlement. Not in one area of life—not within the spirit.

It costs more to have that kind of spirit just as it costs more to wear mink. It means we must cultivate the habit of smiling inside as well as outside. People feel, as well as see, that kind of smile. It means we must cultivate the habit of generosity. Spiritual generosity that makes all with whom you come in contact happy with the world.

It means most of all that you have turned your back upon a veneer. Veneer, you know, makes two pieces of furniture look almost alike. But if you put them side by side after the ravages of time it is the genuine article which is salvageable. It is the true wood which mellows and becomes more beautiful, not the veneer. There must be a depth and sheen far beyond the surface. The wellsprings of your faith are not easy to come by. Each person finds them in his own way. But find them you must if you want to walk as if you were wearing mink.

If you want the genuine rather than the make-do, you can have it. Develop depth to give yourself a sheen. Practice generosity of spirit. Smile deeply enough to put a shine in your eyes.

MINK OR MOUTON? WHICH ARE YOU WEARING TODAY?

Good Form

           * Good form is the easiest type of discipline. So says a member of that professional group which is traditionally associated with temperament and erratic behavior. Good form.

Good form, which means treating those closest to you with the courtesy you grant to those you meet formally. Good form, which means accepting clichés and surface comments with grace when you'd rather scream. Good form, which appreciates the sincerity of friendship's efforts with gratitude. Easy? Easy only if it is habitual. But it is a kind of discipline. That is true.

And we do need to accept it because it is the first step that we can take in the commandment, "Let him deny himself." We need to accept it for another reason, too. Life brings us discipline of a much more severe kind. It may be illness or tragedy or just plain unending struggle. It may be boredom or handicap or simply restrictions which chafe. In this sense then good form is the easiest kind of discipline.

The next time you are tempted to lash out, to explode, to refuse, to ignore, as all of us are at one time or another, think of it as a "denying of self" and it may be easier as experience increases to temper your reactions. Offer your silence as a sacrifice, spiritual and mental. Done in this spirit it will preserve your heart.

> GOOD FORM IS THE EASIEST KIND OF DISCIPLINE. IT WILL HELP YOU TO ENDURE.

As if It Were the Very First Day

* When Barbara Stanwyck, a star who has mastered the ups and downs of her creative world, sent an evaluation of her beliefs for use in an article for youth, one phrase above all others seemed to hold the secret of her success. She said she tried to approach each day's work as if it were her very first day on the job.

Can you think back to your first day on the job? Can you recall the freshness, the magic, the determination you had then to do better than your best? Can you recapture that excitement?

This is, after all, a new day. It is as fresh and untrammeled as a first day would be. You may have to turn your habits upside down but that is sure indication that you need to do so. If you are in the habit of frowning, smile. If you are in the habit of plunging into your work without thinking of the people around you, try saying a happy "Good morning" first. Try to remember just how it was that very first day. A challenge. A joy, with all the dull tasks holding glamour.

Today, whether you are a saleswoman giving service to your customers, a homemaker making breakfast for your family, or an executive facing once more the problems which aren't licked by a time clock, approach your day's work as if it were the very first day.

DYNAMICALLY RECHARGE YOUR SPIRIT. THIS IS THE FIRST DAY.

Over the Mountains

* One of the slivers of satisfaction which came out of the war is that it put faith into "talking" terms. It took religion out of the realm of feminine "do-goodism" and restored it to its rightful place for all men. Few indeed, are the veterans who will not say they felt the Presence at one time or another if they knew combat or saw combat's results. "It's what got me over the mountains, Ma'am," said one private.

Faith has been bringing people over the mountains for a long time now. But that is not the drama nor the test of faith. Its splendor lies in the fact it will take you through the valley, too.

A valley may be the hardest trip of all. From a valley there is no view. Sometimes there is not even the challenge of another mountain ahead. Duty won't sustain you here, nor satisfaction, nor love if it is earthbound.

Faith, alone, can provide that spark of curiosity that makes you want to know the outcome. . . . . . . Knowing you will not see it one moment before you should. . . . . . . Knowing you have not even the right to guess. You have only the right to choose.

CAN YOU SAY, "MY FAITH TOOK ME OVER THE MOUNTAINS. IT WILL TAKE ME THROUGH THE VALLEY, TOO?"

So You Lost the Game

* All of us, at one time or another, have occasion to lose a game. No one minimizes the disappointment of that when it happens. Yet when the excitement of the challenge is over the player who hopes to be ready for a future contest takes time out for evaluation. One of the best questions we can ask ourselves is, "What is a game?" Any game?

It is that contest in which we participate for fun, satisfaction, challenge. Each day we enter a game. We match wits with work, with human relationships, with time. And when we look back it is not the wins and the losses that we so much remember. It is rather the color, the excitement and the challenge of that day.

Without enthusiastic participation there is no game. Unless we use time, it has no value. Do you bring all your skills and a serene sense of confidence to your work? Do you help each person you meet feel prouder for having met you? Does the passing of each hour bring a sense of accomplishment? Could the people watching your performance cheer? Would they want to?

So you lost the game. That will not be what you will remember. What you will remember will be being there.

So you lost the game. . . . . . Or did you?

78

Courage

* It's a word we use unthinkingly all our lives. We associate it with a time of crisis. But courage is a many-faceted gem, not tied to any circumstances, not confined to any pocketbook.

Courage has many shapes and sizes. It can be flamboyant, a physical thing. It can be quietly glowing, a thing of the spirit. Since most of us are not called upon for the spectacular feat we are inclined to underestimate how much of this quality belongs to us.

So what is courage for us? It is bringing a grin to the daily grind. It's the light in the eye on a gray day. It's laughter in the face of fate, amusement at the irony of life. It is a prayer for others when our own need is nearer.

It is saying, "I was mistaken," "I apologize," "I need you." It is finding a rainbow in the soapsuds or the sunlight across the office desk. To be quietly glad about these things is courage.

It is not just in knowing the ladder goes both ways. It is saying so when you've been down as well as up. It is not just in taking a bad fall without a whimper. It is in picking yourself up, with gratitude, instead of pride.

Sometimes it's a gripping hand holding warmth and loyalty. Sometimes its a loosening of the hand, freeing the spirit. It is daily. It is constant. And it is lonely.

But it is lovely, this kind of courage. It gleams, it glows, it flickers. Because it takes faith to show its colors.

COURAGE, LIKE THE SUNRISE, BELONGS TO EVERY DAY.

You Are Lonely, My Friend

* And you can see no good
in loneliness. "If," you say,
"I could only see some purpose in all this."
But you cannot, and your secret self is filled
with bitterness that you should have to stand
alone while others know love and laughter.
Why? Is there a lesson in loneliness?

Because you have known loneliness you
will forever cherish companionship—its
warmth, its depth, its dearness. Not for you,
not ever again, will there be the casual as-
sumption that a moment doesn't matter.

Because you have known loneliness you
will see the tentative flickering light of a
single candle flame of friendship and shield
it quickly from the cold wind of indifference.
Never again will you be too pressed to offer
the supporting hand of loyalty.

Because you have known loneliness you
understand the taste of pain, the bravery of

a smile, the courage of a dream. Because you have the time which loneliness gives, you are aware of the beauty of this world. You sense the tingling promise of the dawn and yearn toward the quiet radiance of the moonlit sky.

You see, my friend, there is a special gift which comes with the experience of loneliness. You learn to savor in a single moment what some do not sense in a lifetime: That life is a gift to be cherished.

BECAUSE YOU HAVE KNOWN
LONELINESS YOU "LIVE"
WHERE OTHERS ONLY EXIST.

Leap to a Laughing Star

    * It's a lovely line, isn't it?

An obscure poet of long ago created it. It came to him in a time that was troubled for its people as we fancy our time is troubled today. It seems, you see, that every age finds its time troubled in one way or another. But a poet "leaps to a laughing star." And you can, too.

The stars are far away and distant, as we see them. Their glitter seems far removed and distant from evil and dismay. But did you ever stop to think that we do not see them except at night? It is the blackness which makes them visible.

Did you ever think of your own difficulties as a black night of accumulation of trials and testings? Did you ever try to put yourself, within your mind, at a point far away and distant, until the things which surround you become pinpoints of light? It is restoring, this perspective.

This kind of faith does demand a leap. It takes a tremendous and mighty surge of faith. But if you land on a laughing star, it's worth it. To yourself and to all those who look to you.

Your night may be fearsome, turbulent, and full of awe. It can also be soft and dark and sweet with rest. It depends upon your leap. It depends upon how often you look up toward the starlight.

ARE YOU TROUBLED? LEAP
TO A LAUGHING STAR.

Leftover Day

    * Any homemaker knows that the lifesaver of the budget is often the leftover bits of food from a sumptuous meal. She knows too that the creativity with which she presents these leftovers governs her family's acceptance of them.

Did you ever ponder upon the fact that we all have leftover day? It may be that moment before twilight and full dark. It may be that residue of time before sleep comes. The way you handle it governs your approach to life, your joy in it, your serenity, and the response of others to you. If you evaluate all the small events with concentration upon gloom, disaster, and the spirit of destruction not only will your day be destroyed but also your tomorrows will be shadowed. People will shy away, for few dare to jeopardize their own serenity by bearing your burdens unless they are too heavy for you to carry alone.

But if you examine your days by concentrating upon the nice moments you will be protecting your spirit and stretching your life. And it is moments we should look for, for a day is made up of minutes. A sudden smile, the pleased pertness of birds bathing in a puddle, the fragrance of amber tea, the sunlit clarity of a busy office with everyone productively sensing their contribution, a choice comment, the peace and softness of the rain—these hold the wonder of the day. These are the moments to remember.

Leftover day. This is the time to remember if you will choose to remember the challenging, enriching moments.

HOW CREATIVE ARE YOU WITH LEFTOVER DAY? IT MAY BE YOUR LIFESAVER.

The Tomorrow Mind

* The constant warnings about the fate of civilization cannot be lightly pushed aside, but neither should they cause us to lose our perspective. Civilization, by its very endurance and its repeated upwelling after apparent obliteration, is more than man's cunning with the tools of life.

There is a spark which has leapt from mind to mind through countless ages and which has forged a golden chain, linking us with the past. It didn't lie in a type or breed. It sprang sometimes from adventurers, it yeasted in explorers, it thundered in scientists, it rested in dreamers. It is the mind of tomorrow.

Kettering put it this way: "Research . . . is a state of mind, going out to look for a change instead of waiting for it to come . . . a composer mind instead of a fiddler mind.

It is the tomorrow mind instead of the yesterday mind."

Through countless eons that spark has existed making today's giants tomorrow's kindergarteners. It shapes today's tragedy into tomorrow's pity; it bears our prideful ingenuity with an indulgent smile. Because of this spark, constant and powerful as the atom, the grandeur of space is not a vast and awesome loneliness. It holds not just the link with the past but the leap toward the future. It holds the mind of tomorrow. So great a conception could only be kindled by the Infinite.

> THE MIND OF TOMORROW IS A FIRE WHICH FORGES A GOLDEN CHAIN. IT IS GOD'S GIFT.

Stand Back

        * One of the finest anti-
dotes to defeatism and dis-
couragement is to cultivate an awareness that
the details of our daily life constitute a big
picture. If you have done any museum hop-
ping you know a painting is always seen best
when viewed from afar.

We all know how repetitious life is. Days
come when you feel you cannot face one more
sinkful of dishes, punch one more time clock,
listen to one more "why," stand one more
hour beside a co-worker. Then it helps to
view the painting from afar; to stand back
and let the fragments fall into place. Suddenly
the perspective is clearer, the shades are
muted, figures spring into view which you in
your nearness had not noted before.

Homemakers have known this from time
immemorial. That is how they are able to
perform so many repetitious tasks with such

equanimity. It helps equally well in the office to think of the pleasure, the ease, the convenience, your work is contributing to others; to appreciate, perhaps, that the troublesome one is the one most skillful with crochety clients; that you are sowing seeds of new thought for a growing generation.

Any work of art is best viewed from a distance. And fruitful living is an art. So when the world presses in, when you become entangled in details, stand back. Stand tall. View your picture from a distance. See how the details blend, how they beautify, how they belong.

> YOUR LIFE IS A PICTURE. STAND BACK TO VIEW IT, THE BETTER TO SEE IT WHOLE.

Cave Man or Christian

      * Do you sometimes knock on wood? Insist that bad luck comes in threes? Shudder when you break a mirror? Then you are saying these things have magical properties. You are reaching away back to the primeval race instincts left in your subconscious mind. . . . . . The instincts cave men obeyed because they knew no better. Our ancestors worshiped trees. In the time of the Wise Men and beyond a cult was built around numbers. Your children know well the place a magic mirror holds in fairy tales.

For generations the unknown has held mystery. But today we pride ourselves upon knowledge. One of the reasons the Christian faith spread like wildfire from its small beginnings was because it released men from old, old fears. How then? How could you deny your Christian faith so dearly won? For that is precisely what you do when you give authority to superstition.

Fear is an insidious thing. It grips the emotions and makes us all children again. The only way we can release that fear is to replace it with an emotion more powerful. There is only one. It is love. The next time you find yourself shivering before a superstition ask yourself, "Am I tossing away so lightly years of dearly bought faith and enlightenment?" Repeat to yourself, "Thou shalt love the Lord thy God . . . with all thy mind."

THE NEXT TIME YOU FIND YOURSELF ABOUT TO KNOCK ON WOOD ASK YOURSELF, CAVE MAN OR CHRISTIAN?

Take a Giant Step

    * Thinking on the obstacles to faith it occurs to us there is no obstacle more stubborn, no barrier higher to climb, than the habit of worry. Reams of words have been written about it and one eye opener puts it this way: If you think carefully about the object of your worries you will discover that you were worrying ten years ago about precisely the same matters you are worrying about today.

That is quite a chunk of time to devote to aimlessness. For isn't aimlessness one facet of the habit of worry? Instead of evaluation, worry; instead of decision, worry; instead of action, worry. It takes just as much concentrated energy to worry as it does to evaluate, decide, act.

Another facet to worry is that it corrodes the quality of our faith. Our Lord at one time said, "Take therefore no thought for the morrow." Since he was not given to impracticalities the implication is clear that he was suggesting we give too much of our hearts to worry and too little to the faith that "your heavenly Father knoweth that ye have need of all these things."

Goethe describes a man who worries as one who takes half steps. Do you recall the game which generations of children have played— Giant Steps? The one who accumulates the most Giant Steps, as opposed to half steps, wins. Half steps. . . . . . Because we are half-hearted about our belief? Could that be?

TODAY TAKE A GIANT STEP
AWAY FROM WORRY.

Cornerstones

* There is a building in our city which has a unique cornerstone. Upon it these words are engraved: To God, for Man. A cornerstone is traditionally the symbolic part of a foundation which supports the entire building. When it is so unequivocally dedicated, it brings a thunderclap of courage to all who pass by.

Whatever we do in life, we need a cornerstone. We need a key square that holds our purpose, our personality, and our spirit in alignment. Have you ever given thought to what your cornerstone might be?

A housewife might ponder the idea that "the hearthstone was the world's first altar." A career girl might remember that the serenest measure of success is the spirit of "the second mile." A businessman might recall in the midst of modern progress the heritage upon which his "today" was built, for certainly an organization which endures proclaims that there was originally a cornerstone of dedicated purpose. Did you ever sit down and evaluate what it might have been? Service? Search? Integrity?

And you, yourself—whatever you may do. Do you have a cornerstone? Is your foundation fabled sand, treacherous in a crisis? Or is it sturdy rock which withstands the storms of a busy and productive life? Is your cornerstone dynamic enough that it brings a thunderclap of courage to all who pass by?

DOES YOUR CORNERSTONE SAY UNEQUIVOCALLY: TO GOD, FOR MAN?